# COVENANT • BIBLE • STUDIES

# In the Beginning

*Wallace Ryan Kuroiwa*

*faithQuest* ◆ Brethren Press

Unless otherwise noted, scripture quotations are from the New Revised Standard Version of the Bible, copyrighted 1989 by the National Council of Churches of Christ in the USA, Division of Education and Ministry.

Cover photo Chris Harvey/Tony Stone Images

97  96  95  94  93          5  4  3  2  1

International Standard Book Number: 0-87178-415-7

Library of Congress Catalog Card Number:  93-72180

Manufactured in the United States of America

# Contents

# Foreword

The Covenant Bible Study Series was first developed for a denominational program in the Church of the Brethren and the Christian Church (Disciples of Christ). This program, called People of the Covenant, was founded on the concept of relational Bible study and has been adopted by several other denominations and small groups who want to study the Bible in a community rather than alone.

Relational Bible study is marked by certain characteristics, some of which differ from other types of Bible study. For one, it is intended for small groups of people who can meet face-to-face on a regular basis and share frankly with an intimate group.

It is important to remember that relational Bible study is anchored in covenantal history. God covenanted with people in Old Testament history, established a new covenant in Jesus Christ, and covenants with the church today.

Relational Bible study takes seriously a corporate faith. As each person contributes to study, prayer, and work, the group becomes the real body of Christ. Each one's contribution is needed and important. "For just as the body is one and has many members, and all the members of the body, though many, are one body, so it is with Christ. . . . Now you are the body of Christ and individually members of it" (1 Cor. 12:12, 17).

Relational Bible study helps both individuals and the group to claim the promise of the Spirit and the working of the Spirit. As one person testified, "In our commitment to one another and in our sharing, something happened. . . . We were woven together in love by the master Weaver. It is something that can happen only when two or three or seven are gathered in God's name, and we know the promise of God's presence in our lives."

The symbol for these covenant Bible study groups is the burlap cross. The interwoven threads, the uniqueness of each strand, the unrefined fabric, and the rough texture characterize covenant groups. The people in the groups are unique but interrelated; they are imperfect and unpolished, but loving and supportive.

The shape that these divergent threads create is the cross, the symbol for all Christians of the resurrection and presence with us of Christ our Savior. Like the burlap cross, we are brought together, simple and ordinary, to be sent out again in all directions to be in the world.

For people who choose to use this study in a small group, the following guidelines will help create an atmosphere in which support will grow and faith will deepen.

1. As a small group of learners, we gather around God's word to discern its meaning for today.
2. The words, stories, and admonitions we find in scripture come alive for today, challenging and renewing us.
3. All people are learners and all are leaders.
4. Each person will contribute to the study, sharing the meaning found in the scripture and helping to bring meaning to others.
5. We recognize each other's vulnerability as we share out of our own experience, and in sharing we learn to trust others and to be trustworthy.

Additional suggestions for study and group-building are provided in the "Sharing and Prayer" section. They are intended for use in the hour preceding the Bible study to foster intimacy in the covenant group and relate personal sharing to the Bible study topic.

Welcome to this study. As you search the scriptures, may you also search yourself. May God's voice and guidance and the love and encouragement of brothers and sisters in Christ challenge you to live more fully the abundant life God promises.

# Preface

Dawn points, and another day
Prepares for heat and silence. Out at sea the dawn wind
Wrinkles and slides. I am here
Or there, or elsewhere. In my beginning.

T.S. Eliot, East Coker, Four Quartets

The thought of beginning something new often excites us, frequently overwhelms us, and sometimes reminds us of what has painfully ended. Yet we are often driven to understand our beginnings, especially the origin of our faith. Even the Bible writers felt compelled to include a statement on primal beginnings—the book of beginnings—Genesis. From its sweeping opening, to the death of Joseph at its close, Genesis rewards its readers with story after story of beginnings of one kind or another: joyful, painful, and hopeful beginnings.

In this study, the first eleven chapters of Genesis command our attention. We attend to some of the most remarkable stories in all of biblical literature, profound stories that reveal who and why we are. As with all truth, these stories mean little unless they are interwoven with our story and our beginnings.

Read these stories with the eyes of your heart and discover the beginning of your faith.

## Recommended Resources:

Brown, Mitchell, and Lee-Lani Wright. "The Story of Beginnings," *A Guide for Biblical Studies*, 108.4 (1993). Elgin, Ill.: Brethren Press.

Brueggemann, Walter. *Genesis* (Interpretation Series). Louisville: Westminster John Knox, 1982.

Carden, John, ed. *A World at Prayer: The New Ecumenical Prayer Cycle*. Mystic, Conn.: Twenty-Third Publications, 1990.

Gibson, John C. *Genesis 1—11*, Vol. 1 (Daily Study Bible-Old Testament Series). Louisville: Westminster John Knox, 1982.

Roop, Eugene F. *Genesis* (Believers Church Bible Commentary). Scottdale, Pa.: Herald Press, 1987.

---

# 1

---

# In the Beginning
### *Genesis 1—11*

*In this opening session, we look at all kinds of begin-
nings in the first eleven chapters of Genesis. In so doing,
we look at the place of beginnings in all our lives, how
they shape our understandings and our visions.*

## Personal Preparation

1. This is the beginning of a study of beginnings! Think about
   the others in your group who will embark with you on this
   study. Take time to pray for each of them, their individual
   needs, concerns, desires, and hopes.
2. One way to read Genesis is as a faith statement. Read the
   opening eleven chapters quickly in one sitting. Jot down
   the statements of faith you see there.
3. According to many scholars, Genesis draws together the
   inspired writings of God's people from several distinct
   periods of history. For a brief explanation of this theory,
   read pages 1-2 of *Interpreter's One-Volume Commentary
   on the Bible* (Nashville: Abingdon Press, 1971).
4. Glance at the other nine chapters in this study of Genesis.
   Note the beginnings studied in each, as well as the issues
   raised.

## Understanding

*Beginning!* What a hopeful word. It promises new horizons. It means embarking on an exciting adventure, charting unbroken territory. As an avid baseball fan, I look forward to the first day of the new season. Anticipation beats in my heart as I consider the possibilities for my favorite team.

Other emotions well up within us as we consider new beginnings. Fear of the unknown often prevents us from starting out. I recall the courage it took to ask a woman to go out with me when I was dating. White-knuckled with anxiety, I stood at the door, hoping she would not answer the doorbell. She came to the door and greeted me with a smile, but I remember the dreadful pause as I tried to muster up the courage to ask her to accompany me to dinner. Tongue-tied and lacking self-confidence, I said something to the effect, "You wouldn't want to go out with me, would you?" A new beginning frequently brings out the worst in us!

One of the most poignant and emotional beginning moments in the history of my people, Japanese Americans, took place at the end of their internment during World War II. After being forced from their homes and coerced to sell their possessions for no reason except that they were Japanese, my people had to begin again. Many had spent the better part of three years behind barbed-wire fences in remote regions. When the camps were dismantled, the prisoners were simply told to leave. One elderly man, angry and defiant at the way they had been treated, refused to leave. He sat on his suitcase as the walls of the camp literally came down around him, and he did not budge. The beginning he was being forced to make did not happen without his protest.

*Genesis* means beginning. It is the Greek word for the first word of the Hebrew text, *bereshith*, translated "in the beginning." The book, as we have it today, is the result of a long process that began in the oral tradition. The stories in the book were first shared by the Jewish people long before anyone thought to write them down. Later on, individuals or groups thought it wise to preserve these stories for future generations in writing. Later still, the stories were collected into what we know as the Book of Genesis from at least three different sources.

Today we can resonate with those individuals who sought to preserve their people's religious traditions. How often I have talked with friends or acquaintances who have felt a need to record their family histories and traditions. Terry Kawata, a good friend and colleague, recently retired as a conference minister in the United Church of Christ. Over lunch one day, I asked about his plans for retirement. I knew he had taken on a challenging interim pastorate, and his experience and gifts made him an excellent resource for the denomination. He said he enjoyed the challenge, but was going to make this pastorate his final official ministry. He wanted to take time to write his family's story. He wanted to leave his children and subsequent generations a remembrance of what pioneer Japanese families in America went through. Although he could have trusted oral tradition to do some of that, Kawata was wise enough to know the story would be passed on more effectively if he wrote it down.

In this study we focus our attention on the first part of Genesis, ending with the call to Abraham in 12:1-3. But it is helpful to understand what follows in chapters 12—50. According to these chapters, the covenant with Abraham produced a special relationship between Israel and God. And according to the covenant agreement, God promised "I will make of you a great nation, and I will bless you, and make your name great, so that you will be a blessing. I will bless those who bless you, and the one who curses you I will curse; and in you all the families of the earth shall be blessed" (12:2-3).

The family of God wondered about their origin, too. When the people of Israel looked back, they realized that the God who had chosen them was the same God who had created the earth! Imagine the magnitude of that revelation as it sank into the consciousness of Israel.

Have you ever wondered why the writers of Genesis included several long genealogies along with the stories? If we understand that the story of the creation of Israel (chapters 12—50) was recorded first and the story of the creation of the world (chapters 1—11) second, we can think of the genealogy as the link between the two stories of beginnings. Genealogies place family beginnings within a wider scope of history. While the linkage is human, the emphasis is on God; the God who made us a people is the Lord of the universe! (Davidson, *Genesis 1—11* [The Cambridge Bible Commentary], 8-9).

Reading Genesis 1—11 this way, we can understand the primal story as a faith statement. Attesting to the richness of God's word,

Genesis can be read in other ways, but we are interested here in the beginning of faith.

Each session of this study looks at a different beginning. Of course, we begin with the beginning of beginnings, the stories of creation. In the two creation narratives, Genesis 1:1—2:4a and 2:4b-25, we find some of the most familiar stories in all the Bible. We will explore not only their relevance for our understanding of the creation of the universe, but also how they can shape our understanding of the world today. The themes of creation will provide ample material for sessions 2 and 3.

In sessions 4-7, we will narrow the spotlight to look at the place of the human in God's creation. We find in the creation narratives powerful stories that address some of the most difficult questions regarding humankind: What is humanity's place in the whole of creation? What do we mean when we claim God creates us in the image of God (session 4)? What conclusions can we draw from the clear claim that God created us male and female (session 5)? In a creation that God ordained good, from where do evil and sin arise (session 6)? How do sin and evil result in broken human relationships (session 7)?

Sessions 8 and 9 call our attention to two of the most challenging stories of prehistory. The great deluge and the story of Noah (session 8) force us to ask more hard questions about human sin and God's judgment. They also give us cause to celebrate hope in God's promise after the flood. Session 9 focuses on that fascinating and curious story of the tower of Babel. Rich in its implications, the story involves us in the attempts of humans to "make a name for themselves."

Finally, session 10 draws us into the simple yet profound way in which God calls a people into being. All the elements of creation are clearly present here: beginning, God's creative word, promise, and hope.

This overview charts the course for our time together. With map in hand, let us begin!

## Discussion and Action

1. People approach beginnings with differing perspectives and emotions. Tell others about one of your important beginnings.

2. How important is family history to you? How difficult is it to record family history accurately? Does the oldest brother or sister in your family remember the family the way the youngest brother or sister does? How do the accounts differ?

3. Look over the beginnings in sessions 2-10. What if they had not happened?

4. These stories of our faith were written by the Jewish people who knew that they were God's chosen people. For them, the creation narratives were full of promise. How would non-Jews understand the creation narratives?

5. All families and clans have powerful and sustaining oral traditions that shape self- understanding. Share with others some of your family stories. How have they helped shape your family's self-understanding? your personal self-understanding?

6. Talk about your expectations of the next nine sessions. Be as open and honest as possible. You can help shape the direction of your study!

# 2

# And It Was Good!
### *Genesis 1:1—2:4a*

*This is the first of two distinct creation stories in Genesis. We rethink this more familiar of the two creation stories as a faith statement. It's clear in Genesis that humankind has a special place in the creation. The author tells us why.*

## Personal Preparation

1. We tend not to read familiar passages from the Bible as carefully as we ought. The passage we concentrate on for this session certainly falls into the category of the familiar. Intentionally read it with a fresh set of eyes, open to new insights.

2. Take time to reflect on the opening session. Recall the hopes and expectations for the course that were shared. As you approach this session, continue to pray for the other members of the group and the issues they raised.

3. This scripture passage has provoked a lot of discussion—often heated—about a human's role and responsibility in the world. Reread the passage and think about what it means for you and your role in the world. Prepare yourself to listen carefully to the varied opinions of others.

4. Of all the ways there are to read this passage, we're interested in its effect as a faith statement. How does Genesis 1:1—2:4a affect your faith?

## Understanding

Kekapa Lee, a Native Hawaiian pastor, once shared a basic tenet of his culture. It is encapsulated in the Hawaiian phrase *aloha 'aina,* the love for the land. Kekapa explained, "Love of the land is a basic Hawaiian cultural value that reminds us that if we take care of the land, the land will take care of us, and we will always have food to eat, water to drink, and a clean place to live. The land also provides us with a sense of belonging, pride, heritage, history, and continuance." And then he shared a Hawaiian proverb: "*He ali'i ka 'aina, he kauwa ke kanaka*" ("The land is chief, we are its servants"). Native Hawaiians, the people who first settled in Hawaii, share similar reverence for creation with their Native American sisters and brothers on the continent. That reverence is familiar to those of the Christian faith, as well.

The writers of Genesis 1:1—2:4a would have shouted amen to the Hawaiian reverence for creation! The powerful and eloquent creedal statement in Genesis attests to the respect and regard with which ancient Israelite people held the created order.

Three mighty affirmations resonate from this magnificent passage (Gen. 1:1—2:4a): God is the Creator, creation is good, and humankind is central in the created order. These affirmations form the elements of the statement of faith. First, the Hebrew community of faith affirmed that God is the creator of all. In this case, the creation is not used as a "proof" for God's existence. God's existence is assumed; one does not need to prove it. As the psalmist observed, "Fools say in their hearts, 'There is no God'" (Psa. 14:1).

When the account says that God speaks the creation into existence ("And God said, 'Let there be . . . ' "), the writer is simply telling us that God wills the creation into being. Moreover, the Creator creates with divine intention, not out of impulse or playfulness, not making it up ad lib. The creation in all its specific aspects arises from the mind of God.

Genesis 1:1—2:4a is not a scientific statement in the modern sense. The writer does not mean to create a consistent, logical, sustainable analysis of how the world came into existence. To the Hebrew culture, the faith to proclaim God the Creator and Sustainer of the universe was more important. In much the same way today, we place faith above knowledge. Recent scientific discoveries about the beginning of the world do not shake our faith in the God who relates to us.

Secondly, this passage affirms the goodness of the creation. Over and over again God responds with approval to creation as it is called into being (vv. 4, 10, 12, 18, 21, 25, 31). But God does not merely watch the order come into being and pronounce it good. God commands the world into being by saying, "Let there be light, water, sky, animals, insects, and human beings." That is to say, God acts. God intends to create. God has a will and a plan.

When God looks at creation and pronounces it good, we know that God's expectations and intentions are fulfilled. There are no mistakes in creation. Everything is complete. It is good. This point is especially important to Native Hawaiians. If the creation gives witness to God's gracious intention, and if God places divine approval on it, then how can we not treat creation with a sense of awe and reverence?

Thirdly, the text clearly gives humankind a major role in the created order. The carefully constructed litany reaches a climax with the final act of creation: "Then God said, 'Let us make humankind in our image, according to our likeness.' " With the creation of the human, God decreed: "And let them have dominion over the fish of the sea, and over the birds of the air, and over the cattle, and over all the wild animals of the earth, and over every creeping thing that creeps upon the earth." In essence, God commands humankind to take a place of prominence and responsibility over the work of divine wisdom and goodness.

The word *dominion* merits some attention here. The Hebrew word used here, *radah*, denotes an absolute royal rule. But this royal rule is patterned after the rule of the one true sovereign, God. In other words, humankind is to rule as God would or, more accurately, in the image of God. In fact, God's command to tend the earth is combined with the discussion of how we are made in God's image (1:26-31).

Isaiah 11:3-5 tells us more specifically how God rules and, therefore, how we are to rule over creation. First of all, the ruler delights in faith. The one who has dominion over the created order should have faith, remembering that it was God who brought about the created order. The ruler is also just and righteous, never tyrannical or unfair. The ruler pays special attention to the poor and the meek, ensuring that the needs of all are cared for.

I like to think of God's command to have dominion as an instruction about stewardship. The earth and all things in it belong to God (Psa. 24:1). When God gives us the responsibility of stewardship, God commands us to act as caretakers over the divine estate. It is not for our use, but it is ours to manage and tend. Caring for creation elevates our sense of humility, not our pride. We will take greater care of our world, knowing it belongs to God and that we are accountable to God. Our dominion over God's creation, then, requires us to exercise this power justly and with loving care, not capriciously, in self-serving, exploitative ways.

Even as this study is being put together, millions of people are becoming more and more concerned about the environment. From the family who recycles to the international leaders who gather for an environmental summit, fear for the creation has reached crisis proportions. Global warming, destruction of the ozone layer, air and water pollution top a crowded agenda. Sadly, we have reached a point of having to do damage control. We can't think of cleaning up the world before first slowing the rate of destruction. We have done a poor job of exercising dominion over all the earth. We have not been just rulers over our given realm.

As a Japanese American, I have grown up with a love for bonsai, the art of shaping in miniature that which nature creates. Bonsai, like much of Japanese art, comes from philosophy. By creating a miniature environment in which the plant is to grow and by careful shaping, we produce a miniature of nature. Bonsai teaches us that nature and its Creator are the master artists, and we can create beauty and life by following their example, not by doing what *we* feel is best.

In conclusion, Genesis 1:1—2:4a is the study of a beginning. We see in it, not only a beginning in terms of time, but in terms of a foundation. It informs us of God's intentions, the success of those intentions, and how we as humans are to participate in carrying out his intentions. What an awesome responsibility and privilege!

## Discussion and Action

1. Listen to the text as someone reads it aloud. Share what this text says to you about God.
2. The opening chapter of Genesis affirms our faith in the goodness of creation. On newsprint or sheet of paper, list the things that are good about creation. Save the list for later in this session.

3. As stewards of the earth, how are we to care for the earth? Talk about the difference between ruling over creation and tending creation. How are they alike?

4. How is the truth in a faith statement different from the truth in a scientific statement? Do you need proof for faith?

5. Talk about the concerns your group has about the state of the environment. Write down those concerns on slips of paper to be used later.

6. Envision the kind of world you want to leave to your children. Discuss what it will take to work toward that kind of world. What keeps you from working on these issues now? Make a plan as a group to do something for the environment. For instance, volunteer at the recycle center, plant trees in the church yard, or pick up trash in the neighborhood around the church.

7. Conduct a short worship service. Here is a suggested order of worship:

> Hymn:
>> "I Sing the Mighty Power of God"
>
> Prayer:
>> Offer sentence prayers praising God for the good things in creation using the list prepared in number 2.
>
> Unison or dramatic reading of Psalm 8
>
> Intercessory Prayer:
>> Using the slips of paper created in number 5, have one person read the concern and every-one respond with "For this, we lift our hearts in prayer."
>
> Silent reflection
>
> Hymn:
>> "God of the Earth, the Sky, the Sea"

# 3

# Remember the Sabbath
## *Genesis 2:1-4a*

*God rested on the sabbath, not out of exhaustion, but to survey what had been done and to celebrate it. God's example gives us cause to examine the place of sabbath in our lives.*

## Personal Preparation

1. This session focuses on sabbath. Read the passage and reflect on the importance of sabbath in your life. How do you observe the sabbath? How did you observe it as a child? How would you like to observe the sabbath?
2. Ask some of your friends how they observe sabbath. If you know someone who is Jewish, Seventh-day Adventist, or a Jehovah's Witness, ask them how and when they observe sabbath.
3. Think of your own experiences of legalistic attitudes, either your own or other's, about sabbath. How do you respond to them?
4. How do you observe or find sabbath during the week?

## Understanding

I once heard a story about a missionary who was guided up the Amazon River by some of the native people there. The missionary needed to meet someone and was anxious to proceed as fast as possible. A few days into the trek and eager to finish, he came upon the native guides sitting together, obviously unwilling to go on. When he asked the interpreter what was causing the delay, the missionary got a revealing reply: "They are waiting. They cannot move farther until their souls have caught up with their bodies." I would venture to say that most of us know that feeling of not having our lives together. If for no other reason, the practice of sabbath is necessary just to "keep body and soul together."

Many of us regret the loss of a peaceful, relaxed lifestyle. Our lives are becoming faster paced, and many of us don't like that. The creation story helps us understand more fully why we sense a loss of peace. The story of the seven days of creation reminds us that God built into the natural order one day that is different from the rest. When we fail to set apart time from the usual routine, we have violated God's natural order.

The narrator in the scripture notes that God did not rest on the seventh day because of fatigue after the magnificent work of creation. Rather, God rested to make this day holy (v. 3). The word *holy* here means "setting apart." The sabbath was to be a day different from all the rest, a day to sit back and look out upon the world with satisfaction in the creation and give thanks for what was done.

The divine command to observe the sabbath can be found in both versions of the Ten Commandments. In Exodus 20:8, the writer remembers that God gave us an example to follow, setting aside the seventh day after creation and instructing us to keep the sabbath holy because God did. The work of creation is complete, toil stops, and we take time to celebrate the creation God has made.

Deuteronomy 5:13-15 also commands sabbath observance, with a slightly different rationale. Here we are commanded to remember that God brought Israel out of slavery. "Remember that you were a slave in the land of Egypt, and the Lord your God brought you out from there with a mighty hand and an outstretched arm; therefore the Lord your God commanded you to keep the sabbath day" (Deut. 5:15). In their still vivid memory of bondage in Egypt, the Hebrews recalled the oppression in which the Egyptians "made their lives bitter with hard service in mortar and brick and in every kind of field labor" (Exod. 1:14), a labor so backbreaking the "Israelites groaned under their slavery, and cried out" (Exod. 2:23). Thus, the sabbath law commanded them to remember their extreme toil and God's justice, which saved them.

Rest after creation and God's justice also shape how we observe the Sabbath. As Christians we reserve one holy day each week to look back on and celebrate God's creation. We also give thanks for God's justice, which "delivers us from evil" and "forgives us our debts."

But we must remember that we have not reached unanimity about what the example of God's sabbath means for us. What exactly did God mean by setting apart a special day? We struggle with the implications of the fourth commandment. What does the word *rest* require? What about exceptions in unusual circumstances? How long should the sabbath last? At times we have answered these questions by making rules: do not work on Sunday, do not shop on Sunday, do not go to movies on the sabbath.

In Jesus' day, some religious leaders also applied sabbath restrictions to literally hundreds of acts, including acts of necessity and mercy. Jesus found himself in trouble with those religious authorities, because he took the sabbath to be a day of remembrance of mercy and justice, not a day of prohibitions. When he led the disciples through the grainfield, picking grain to feed his hungry followers, the Pharisees charged him with violating the sabbath, but Jesus reminded them that acts of justice override the law, such as the time when David fed forbidden bread to his hungry companions on the sabbath (Matt. 12:1-8).

We delight that at times Jesus tripped up the Pharisees in their legalisms. But which one of us has been entirely true to the sabbath? If we do not have strong convictions about what is or is not proper to do on Sunday, we often err on the other side, failing to do much at all to make the sabbath a celebration of creation or mercy. Sunday is just another shopping day, a day off, interrupted by church services that we hope won't keep us past the kickoff of the big game. We take care of obligatory family visits and change the oil in the car if there is time. We have made the sabbath into a routine, a day that is different only in the kind of toil or activity we pursue.

The debate over how to observe sabbath is not new. Christians have wrestled with how to keep the sabbath for centuries. In U.S. history, puritan Christians spent long hours in worship and the rest of the sabbath in their homes, refraining from work. Sometimes they would even schedule "lectureships" on Sunday afternoon to fill the void between morning services and evening prayers.

More recently, Eric Liddell, whose life was the subject of the movie *Chariots of Fire*, was a world class athlete who was favored to win several events in the Olympics. He gave up his place in an important qualifying race because it was scheduled for Sunday. Racing on Sunday ran counter to his deep conviction for keeping the sabbath.

Some Christian groups have experimented with the sabbath idea of letting land rest every seven years. If anything grows in the fields without human attention, it is available to all. Others such as Koinonia Farms and Jubilee Partners model themselves after the sabbath practice of declaring a year of Jubilee every fiftieth year, redistributing land and wealth. They apply sabbath broadly to the whole creation.

What does this mean for us as heirs of the long struggle to interpret the sabbath? Let me draw two conclusions for us. First, God created the sabbath as part of the natural order of things. The Creator did not make the sabbath out of necessity; God did not rest because of fatigue. Neither did God simply act as a role model, resting so that by observing, we would learn and follow. No, I believe the sabbath is rooted in the rhythm of the universe. The regularity of the seasons, the invariable sunrise and sunset, and the completely predictable cycle of birth, life, and death attest to the rhythm of creation and the total reliability of God. God created the world with all its rhythm and balance in six days and then created a seventh day to look back with satisfaction. With the same regularity, we look back at the way that creation sustains us and give thanks for God's handiwork.

Second, the sabbath is part of being human, part of being created in the image of God who is a righteous and just ruler (see session 2). The God who created the natural order sustains us, protects us, and delivers us with mercy and justice. We, in turn, observe the sabbath and take on the image of God when we are just and merciful. Sabbath calls us to regularly feed the hungry, restore land to the poor, and allow everyone to rest from their labor. And every seventh day and every seventh year we remember God's mercy and justice so that we will be merciful and just, too.

In the end, sabbath has more to do with the image of God than with fulfilling the physical need to rest. We fulfill sabbath when we celebrate creation and show mercy. While relaxing and resting are necessary, they do not fulfill sabbath by themselves. Worship that reflects and remembers the source of life, grace, and justice is sabbath. Recreation that helps us appreciate the created order is sabbath. Merciful rest after hard work is sabbath. A break from our sometimes slavish jobs to spend time with family is sabbath.

The sabbath is God's gift of grace to us. It is a time to celebrate our love of God, family, friends, and our community of faith. Walking with my son, reading to my daughter, having a private dinner and conversation with my wife redeem me from the demands of work and other people. I am free to be joyful for the life God gives me. Sabbath is my gift of faith to the God of creation and mercy.

## Discussion and Action

1. Read Genesis 2:1-4a aloud.
2. How do you observe sabbath now? What would you like to change, and how would you make those changes?
3. Do you agree that God created the sabbath for celebrating creation and mercy and justice? How does rest figure into the sabbath for you? What do you do on the sabbath to celebrate creation and justice?
4. Talk about the ways others observe the sabbath. Tell how you observed the sabbath as a child. What do you miss about the sabbath of your childhood? What changes in sabbath observance please you?
5. How can you help each other to slow down, to spend more time in sabbath? How can the congregation encourage members to observe sabbath?
6. Be silent for a few minutes, praying for internal peace and rest from the hectic day. Take a sabbath moment and think about what you are grateful for in creation. Close by having someone read John Greenleaf Whittier's verse:

> O Sabbath rest by Galilee!
> O calm of hills above,
> Where Jesus knelt to share with Thee
> The silence of eternity,
> Interpreted by love.

---

# 4

---

# In God's Image
### *Genesis 1:26-27*

*This poetry tells us that only humans are created in the "image of God." In this session we will look at the way we are made that sets us apart from the rest of the created order.*

## Personal Preparation

1. This session focuses on the creation of humanity. It asks us to consider the wonder of this aspect of God's creation. As you meditate and pray in preparation for this session, read Psalm 8. Allow the sense of awe in the psalm to permeate your spirit.
2. Reflect on what it means to be made in God's image. How does the image of God set us apart from the rest of creation?
3. Watch the news and read newspapers and magazines for stories that affirm or deny the image of God in us. Be prepared to share these in the Bible study.

## Understanding

I experienced the late Sixties as a seminary student in the San Francisco Bay Area. I often quip that I received as much of an education—if not more—from living in that environment as from going to classes. The riots at the University of California-Berkeley, flower children, San Francisco State, pot, psychedelic music and art, dropping out, and other parts of the counterculture characterized the hope of the generation. As much as anything, a new optimism about the goodness and possibilities of humankind marked that era. I can still remember walking in the Haight-Ashbury district of the city, where the flower children held forth, and seeing a young hippie give a flower to a police officer who had just ordered people not to loiter.

In those days, a musical group called Jefferson Airplane recorded an album entitled *Crown of Creation* that spoke powerfully to the youth of the day, who believed they had the power to change the establishment. The album portrayed humankind as the height, the best of God's creation. It understood humans to have the image of God imprinted deep in their souls.

Genesis 1:26-27 clearly asserts the uniqueness of humankind. It tells us God created humankind as the culmination of the creative process. But what does it mean to be created in God's image? Obviously, we can never know with absolute certainty what it means. Biblical scholars have studied the meaning of this sentence, but they don't all agree with each other! No one has found the key that unlocks the mystery.

One particular viewpoint on the image of God makes sense to me. This understanding contrasts that part of human nature we call the image of God with the part of ourselves we consider creaturely. Our creatureliness is the part of us that is bound to the natural environment. The natural world, with its laws, limits, and capacities, places limitations upon us. For instance, we cannot be in two places at the same time, we cannot survive without food and water, we are all finite and will die.

The image of God, on the other hand, addresses our capacity to transcend the limits placed upon our creatureliness by nature. We can make choices. We have will and can shape our environment or even change it. We have purposes toward which we live. And we are creatures that relate to God and to each other.

The text from Genesis makes the claim that we are both creature and image of God. God creates us; we are creature. And yet God creates us distinct from the rest of creation. In the first volume of his book *Nature and Destiny of Man*, American theologian Reinhold Niebuhr said that sin comes from emphasizing one or the other, creatureliness or godlikeness, too much. Affirming the image of God in us while denying our creatureliness results in the sin of pride.

Accepting our creatureliness at the cost of denying the image of God leads to the great excuse, "I'm only human!"

Augustine, a bishop in North Africa in the fifth century, added a very important concept to our understanding of the image of God. He believed that our capacity to return God's love is a reflection of the divine. Love comes from free will, and free will, being one of those traits that is not confined by the natural world, is a divine trait. God loves us freely, and we love God freely.

God creates us not only with the capacity for relating to others in love, but also with the need for relationship. If there were no need for relationship, Genesis might have reported the creation of one being, but Genesis reports the creation of *two* beings. God created two different beings whose relationship brought together their various gifts, traits, talents, and strengths. Relationship draws complementary characteristics together, creating a whole. Maleness and femaleness bring our opposite natures together in one complete union.

God also finds completion in the Word. John 1:1-4 tells us that God was not alone, even in the beginning, before the earth was formed. The Word was fully with God, and the Word was God. Then God made humankind at the culmination of creation. We were beings to whom God could relate and who were the image of God. This relational God is pained by our unfaithfulness and pleased by our fidelity. God hears our cries and receives our praise. God makes covenants with us and promises to protect us. And we find our completion and meaning in God.

Despite the very personal nature of God reflected in human beings, it is risky to try to find God's image in the physical characteristics of individuals. Since individuals themselves are incomplete, some scholars think it is unlikely that the writer of Genesis saw the image of God in a person. More likely God's image is present in humankind as a whole. Comparing this view to the way the Apostle Paul talked about the body (1 Cor. 12:12-31), we are the body of Christ only when we come together as a whole, combining our various gifts. Then we can talk generally about humankind's capacity to love, the ability to have dominion, and the need to relate to others and to God.

These emphases point us to the wonder of the Genesis declaration that God creates us in the divine image. How can we not break out into song with the psalmist who said, "What are human beings that you are mindful of them, mortals that you care for them? Yet you have made them a little lower than God, and crowned them with glory and honor. You have given them dominion over the works of your hands; you have put all things under their feet . . ." (Psa. 8:4-6).

## Discussion and Action

1. Read Psalm 8. In what ways are we made in the image of God?
2. Share the news stories and other reports from question 2 in Personal Preparation that affirm or deny the image of God in us.
3. It is very difficult to maintain the balance between being too prideful and too humble. Talk about the paragraph on Reinhold Niebuhr. How do you strike a balance?
4. What, in your opinion, makes a good relationship? How does your relationship with God model the way people should relate?
5. What evidence is there in our society or our world that humankind is made in God's image? What can a society do to reflect God's image that an individual cannot?
6. End the session with sentence prayers. In your prayers, take time to pray for specific ways in which we as a global community can better express the image of God within us.

# 5

# Man and Woman
## *Genesis 2:4b-25*

*This is the second creation story, very different from the first. It is a carefully constructed account of the creation of man and woman and their sexual distinctions. A careful reading shows that this passage supports equality—the sexes are separate but equal.*

## Personal Preparation
1. The reading for this session begins a new account of the creation. Read 1:1—2:4a as a whole, and then read 2:4b-25. List the order in which things are created in each story, then compare your lists. How do you explain the repetition (for example, the repetition of the creation of humans)? Did you find differences in the accounts? How do you explain those differences? Why do you think we have two stories of creation?
2. Which account of creation is more familiar to you? Read the less familiar story several times this week.
3. What is your understanding of why God created man and woman? Jot down your answer and then read the lesson. Would you change your answer or leave it the same? If your answer has changed, how?

## Understanding

The Kuroiwa clan recently met for their annual reunion. We had stopped having the reunions after the six Kuroiwa brothers who came from Japan to Hawaii died. But three years ago a group of us decided we needed to resurrect the annual bash, and most of the folks got together for a grand reunion. We ate, had games for the youngsters, saw who had babies since our last meeting, and generally had a good time. It felt so good, in fact, we decided we would try to do it every year on the second Sunday in August.

Part of the magic of these reunions—and all family reunions, for that matter—lies in the fact that we are able to tell our family stories. In gathering we share our history with one another, recalling who we were and how it was. We share these stories with our children and their children, because we want the power of these stories to be preserved for generations to come.

The stories we read in Genesis 2:4b-25 are, in a sense, the stories of the human family. They were told over and over long before they were written down in a book. Readers of the two creation stories (Gen. 1:1—2:4a and Gen. 2:4b-25), however, will notice that one story is quite different from the other story. The grand, rhythmic verses of the first creation account have a different quality than the "earthy," more storylike style of the second. Moreover, the watery chaos of Genesis 1 is replaced by the arid, desertlike conditions in which the creation takes place in Genesis 2.

But beyond these noteworthy contrasts in style and setting, the stories have at least two major theological distinctions. First of all, humans have a very central place in the second account. From the beginning of the creation in Genesis 2:4b-25, God creates the human animal out of the arid wasteland, giving human beings a more central role in God's world. Whereas, in the story of the seven days of creation (the first account), humankind is not made until the sixth day.

Secondly, the story in Genesis 2:4b-25 gives us greater detail about man and woman. In the earlier account, man and woman represent humankind generally. But in the second account, God distinguishes between the sexes and makes them equally important, although they are different. In her book *God and the Rhetoric of Sexuality*, Phyllis Trible explores the two important differences.

Trible says that God clearly puts the human at center stage in the creation. In the order of creation, God makes the human being first

(2:7) and puts this person in the garden to tend it (2:15). Then God creates the animals for the person (2:19-20). After the animals prove unsatisfactory for God's purposes and the person's needs, God performs divine surgery and creates a partner for the human (2:21-22).

Clearly, the humans stand on center stage throughout the creation drama. But, in contrast to the first creation story, no language of dominion appears. Yes, God does create the flora of the garden and places humans in its midst; and yes, animals find their original purpose in meeting human need; but the story is told in such a way as to minimize the notion that the creation is here for our dominion. Humankind is important simply because God wants people to have pleasure in and enjoy the creation. We are important because God values us, not just our strengths.

Trible also talks about the creation of sexual distinctions. Very few biblical texts have been used more frequently than this one to show why women should be subordinate to men. From it many have reasoned that God created man first and woman last, assuming first is superior and last is inferior; also, that woman is created as helper for man and thus is subordinated; and woman was created from man's rib and therefore owes her existence to him. And so on.

A careful reading of the text, Trible says, negates such arguments. The word used in the Hebrew text for the human creature is *ha-adam*. Ha-adam is created by God out of the dust of the earth (*ha-adama*), and when God breathes into the dust, ha-adam becomes a living creature. The use of the word *ha-adam* is translated in most English translations as "the man," but the Hebrew language clearly does not make the word gender-specific. Only later in the text do "male" and "female" appear.

The distinction between man and woman takes place only after God has found the creation of animals to be unsatisfactory as a partner for ha-adam, who up to this point has no gender (v. 20). So God causes a deep sleep to fall upon ha-adam and performs divine surgery, taking a rib from ha-adam and closing the flesh (v. 21). God then takes the rib and creates out of it woman and brings her to ha-adam (v. 22). In joy, ha-adam says, "This at last is bone of my bones and flesh of my flesh; this one shall be called Woman (*ishshah*), for out of Man (*ish*) this one was taken" (v. 23). What we do find here is the beginning of sexual distinction. Ha-adam only becomes male when the female is created. And he has a male identity only in that he is different from the female, not better or worse. The order of creation of male and female is not sequential; it is simultaneous.

Notice first of all that this woman is a new creation. In all the previous creative acts of this account, God takes the earth and forms from it ha-adam, the plants, and the animals. Here God uses the rib of ha-adam and creates woman from it. But to be made of the rib in no way signifies inferiority. It is, rather, something very unique.

Secondly, as Trible points out, God the divine Matchmaker brings woman to ha-adam in a distinct way. Previously, God had placed ha-adam in the garden to till it and keep it (v. 15). Then God brought the animals to ha-adam for the purpose of naming them. But here God does not create another creature over whom the man can have dominion. The purpose seems to be to create someone to alleviate loneliness and solitariness. Woman comes as a helpmate, or rather, the two become helpmates to each other. It is not another creature just like himself that man needs, but someone who provides the things he is not. Woman is man's complement. In their relationship they help each other to be fully human—strong and compassionate, keepers and tenders of creation. Trible asks us not to think of helper as a subordinate partner, but a mutual one.

Phyllis Trible has given us a whole new way of looking at the roles of man and woman, a very powerful way. If we accept it, we may assume that the order of creation is not important, helpmates are not subordinate, and being made of the rib is not inferior. We may also assume that God intended man and woman to be partners in creation, loving and serving each other. Here again we pick up the theme of relationship and God's intent that we relate to each other just as our personal God relates to us.

Like all good stories, this creation story endures because in it we find truth and power. As we leave this portion of the story, we have a new purpose and excitement. We will return to earth in the next chapter.

## Discussion and Action

1. As a group, list from memory the events of creation. Then compare your list to the biblical accounts. Did you combine events from both stories into one? Did you list anything that is not in the biblical account?

2. Compare your responses and reflections from question 1 in Personal Preparation. Do you all respond differently to the two accounts of creation?
3. What would we be missing if there was only one creation story? Why are both needed?
4. Share your understanding of why God created man and woman. Has your understanding changed over your lifetime? How?

# 6

# In the Garden
## *Genesis 3*

*In the story of beginnings, we eventually get to the bad part, the fall. But the fall is not the story of just one couple in the garden. It is the story of our own temptation, disobedience, guilt, denial. The good news is that it is also the story of God's grace, which overcomes our sin and helps us grow.*

## Personal Preparation

1.  The creation story that begins with 2:4b-25 continues here. Read 2:4b—3. How does the relationship between the man and the woman change between chapter 2 and chapter 3? Jot down your observations to share with the rest of the group.
2.  In what ways can you identify with the woman and man? In what ways do you feel distant from them?
3.  This is also a story of maturation and growth. Reflect on a first-time experience from your adolescence. What was exciting about it? What was painful? What did you learn?

## Understanding

When I watch the television series "Wonder Years," I feel as if I'm revisiting my youth in the 1950s and '60s. The show explores in humorous and sometimes painful ways the burgeoning awareness of life, love, and intimacy. Kevin, the adolescent character around whom the show revolves, discovers what it means to grow into adulthood.

Much of the show's magic for me comes from Kevin's first time experiences: first love, first driver's license, first rejection. All of us can share stories that rival the ones on "The Wonder Years." Our stories may be ecstatic, painful, nostalgic. They are our unique stories, but in hearing them, others nod and affirm them. They can say, "I can relate to that; I know just what you mean."

Genesis 3 is also the story of first things: the first disobedience, first knowledge, first awareness of the self, first choice. Like the "The Wonder Years," the story is universal. It not only speaks to generations past, it speaks equally effectively to generations of the future, our generation. With the stories of the fall, the storyteller in Genesis brings us face to face with our attempts, our failures, and our growing edges.

Traditionally, we emphasize the negative aspects of the garden story, beginning with temptation embodied in the serpent. As scholars point out, the serpent is more cunning than evil. It is able to outwit the pair of humans, drawing them into disobedience. The text does not suggest anywhere that the serpent symbolizes the devil. That idea surfaces in interpretations of this passage. Contrary to the interpretations, however, the serpent in our story is identified as one of God's creatures.

Notice how the serpent tempts every faculty of the woman. It begins by tempting her intellect: "Did God say, 'You shall not eat from any tree in the garden'?" The serpent's question is actually an effort to get the woman to doubt in her mind. Next, the serpent tempts the woman's desire for power: eat and you will be like God. Then the serpent appeals to the physical senses: the woman saw that the fruit "was a delight to the eyes." Succumbing to the overwhelming force of temptation, she and the man ate.

A second negative aspect of the story is disobedience. The primal pair chooses to go beyond the limits set by God. The pair was made in the image of God. As Augustine suggests, God created them with the capacity to return the love of God; but the choice to act against God's will results in the fall. Out of a desire to love and be loved, God risked giving humans choice. But the humans choose to misuse their freedom and disobey. As the saying goes, the problem was not so much the apple in the tree (temptation) as it was the pair on the ground!

Thirdly, we emphasize guilt and denial. When woman and man hear God, they hide, feeling guilty for their disobedience. They do not hearken to the voice they once revered. And when God does discover their disobedience, they rationalize their actions. They refuse to accept responsibility for what they have done. The man blames the woman; the woman blames the serpent.

The traditional interpretations of the Garden of Eden rarely emphasize the positive side of the fall. Man and woman lose their innocence but they gain knowledge. Created in God's image, human beings have choice and free will, which they use poorly at times. But it is only through choice and free will that we grow and mature. Like woman and man in the garden, we test the limits, we make our choices, and in the end we gain knowledge. Knowledge is often painful, but the process of maturing is rewarding. Growing to maturity is growing into our full personhood, into the image of God.

We don't make poor choices deliberately to learn a lesson—like smashing up the car. But we do take chances, hoping something will come of it. We risk expressing love for someone hoping they'll reciprocate. Even when they don't return love, we try again.

God responds to Adam and Eve's risk of disobedience without being vengeful or punitive. The judgment is God's way of saying that our actions have consequences. Living with the results of our bad choices is punishment enough: "Because you have done this . . ." (v. 14, and implied in 16, 17). This tragic story actually ends on a hopeful note. Judgment is not the final word; grace is. The divine Tailor makes clothes for the banished pair (v. 21). Then he sends them to a protected place and cares for them despite their willful disobedience.

We have judged man and woman in the Garden of Eden perhaps more harshly than God did. We may be kinder to them if we can see ourselves in them. The weaver of this story is trying to tell us that we recreate the fall over and over in our individual lives. We are Adam; we are Eve. Like Kevin on "The Wonder Years," we have our eyes opened in the experiences of discovery and awakening, even when we willfully disobey God.

Woman most of all has been held responsible for the fall. Tradition has us believing that the woman is the only culprit, the one who is singlehandedly responsible for the fall. After all, does she not converse with the serpent? Does she not pluck the fruit and offer it to the man?

But consider what is said and not said in the text. The man is surely present during the dialogue between the serpent and the woman, yet he remains silent and passive. When the woman offers the fruit to him, nothing in the text suggests that she fools him or seduces him to take the fruit. His response to her offer is largely from his stomach and encapsulated in three words: "and he ate." He is just as aware of the divine prohibition as she. Yet he does not hesitate to do as the woman does: he eats. And exile is handed out as punishment to both man and woman, which suggests that both are guilty.

What if, in fact, woman acted alone and is responsible for man's ruin? Can she then also be credited with the positive aspects of the fall? Like God, who took the risk of giving humans free will, the woman took the risk of exercising her will, hoping to become closer to God. She is the one who thirsts for knowledge and growth. She wants to become fully human *and* live in the image of God. God, who until now has provided everything for the couple, takes away their innocence. In the end, God is still the provider when he banishes man and woman from the garden and their naiveté and puts them east of Eden where they will always be protected. We blame woman for sin but fail to recognize her as the one who won God's unfailing protection for us.

The story of the fall is recreated in us all. In my God-given freedom, I choose self over God. I disobey. I feel guilt and deny it. I hide from God. I cause the repercussions of my sin, whether I feel them directly or whether they are felt by others. My eyes are opened and I see my nakedness. I cannot blame some primordial pair in some idyllic garden long ago and far away. The sin, with its power and strength, its consequences and shame, is mine alone.

Nevertheless, even as we must bear responsibility for our sins, we also receive God's grace. If we are to hear the gospel in all its fullness, we must hear the word of judgment as merely the penultimate word, the second to the last word. For the last word is grace. In the same way that God provided for the primordial pair in the garden, God offers grace to all of us. God does not simply say, "You made your bed, go sleep in it." The overwhelming testimony of the gospel paints God as the rescuer (Hosea and Gomer, for example), the forgiving parent (Jesus' parable of the Unforgiving Brother), and the seeking shepherd, to name just a few examples. As much as the cross stands as judgment on our sins, it also portrays a God who "so loved the world."

## Discussion and Action

1. Share your feelings of identification with Adam and Eve. Also share your feelings of distance from them. Do you agree with the author that "We are Adam; we are Eve"?
2. The writer describes the experience of Adam and Eve as one of discovery and awakening. Reflect together on what they lose. What do they gain? Share a time when you took a risk. What did you lose or gain?
3. Reflect on "passing the buck." How do you behave when you are rightfully accused of doing wrong? How do you wish you would behave?
4. When have you experienced grace after making a wrong decision? Have you ever made a bad decision, knowing you would be forgiven anyway? If we're always forgiven, what is the real consequence of sin?
5. Sing one verse of "Amazing Grace," and close the session with sentence prayers. Focus your prayers on confession. At the conclusion of the prayer time, have someone read 1 John 1:9.

# 7

# Where Is Your Brother?
## *Genesis 4:1-16*

*This story addresses the question of the seeming inequity of God's blessing. God favors Abel's offering over Cain's. And instead of railing against God, Cain takes his anger out on Abel, killing him. The themes of rage, jealousy, and violence are consequences of the fall.*

## Personal Preparation

1. This story reveals some of the most powerful human emotions we experience. Many of the emotions Cain feels are a reaction to God's favor for Abel (4:4b). As you think about this story, consider the inequities in your personal life and in the world. How do you react to these inequities?
2. Do a comparative reading of this story with the story of the fall in Genesis 3. What do they have in common? How are they different?
3. Think of responsibilities you have had for others? How did you feel about your responsibilities?

## Understanding

One of the great lines about the ability of the poor to endure poverty and even laugh at it comes from the musical *Fiddler on the Roof.* Tevye, the main character, is a Russian Jew, a poor farmer. God has blessed him with a wonderful family, but little else. Contemplating his meager existence, he talks to God in song.

"There is no shame in being poor," he tells the Almighty, "but it is no great honor, either!"

How many of us would shout amen to that! How many of us, seriously or jokingly, have commented about the inequitable distribution of material goods in the world? Why do some possess so much and others so little? Why does approximately one-fourth of the world control ninety percent of the world's goods? Why do people starve in a world in which there is enough food to feed everyone sufficiently?

From our vantage point as citizens of a bountiful country, we are sometimes tempted to believe that our abundance is a blessing. But that somehow implies that the impoverished people of the world are cursed and that we are somehow better than others because we have the good fortune of being born here. It also raises questions about God. Does God favor some people more than others?

The story before us in Genesis 4 addresses the problem of God's unequal favor. Cain, the "tiller of the ground," and his brother Abel, the shepherd, bring their offerings to God. The storyteller reports that God is pleased with Abel's offering but has "no regard" for Cain's. The narrative does not give a reason for God's discrimination. In his rage, Cain lures his younger brother out into the field and kills him.

This tragic story shares much with the story of the fall. Both stories feature sin, a God who searches for us, a sinner who hides, judgment, and grace. But several elements make this story unique. In the story of the two brothers, the reader struggles with the problem of God's unequal favor. Why does God favor one brother's offering over the other? This question has perplexed people of faith for generations. The narrator does not report a lack of faith, unrighteous behavior, or improper motives as reasons. Try as we might to discover some rationale for God's response, we have to admit that any reason we think of is simply a guess. God's reasons are hidden from human knowledge.

We can find an interesting parallel to this story in a much later book of the Bible, the story of Job. Job, too, feels God has rejected him. Like Cain, Job cannot understand why. But Job and Cain respond to God's mysterious acts in two very different ways. Cain is immediately filled with rage (v. 5b), while at first Job reacts in faith: "Though he slay me, yet will I trust in him" (Job 13:15 KJV)

Obviously, Job models the reaction to God we hope we would have when faced with seeming injustice. But Job also experiences doubts and anger and lashes out at God. A perfect understanding did not guide Job through his crisis.

Inequities occur in all areas of life, personal and social. One country suffers drought, famine, poverty; another enjoys full larders and life-giving rains. Why? Does God favor one over the other? If so, rage is a natural and understandable response. We protest against a God who has a hand in what happens in the world and lets people suffer for no apparent reason.

This is Cain's way. He rages. But instead of railing against God, Cain takes it out on his brother. Cain's actions take an irrational turn at this point. Again a comparison with Job might prove helpful. Job feels anger at God because he believes God has directed action against him. But he goes directly to God and rails against God, asking for a hearing at the divine court. He even voices his doubt that God will oblige him, but God does hear him and humors his request.

Cain, by contrast, looks for revenge against God by assaulting someone else. He conspires in his heart to kill his brother, who, as far as we know, has nothing to do with determining God's favor. Abel, along with Cain, simply brought his offering to God, and God chose one over the other. Cain allows his rage to alienate him from both God and his brother. Cain acted upon his jealousy. His feelings, natural as they may have been, did not justify his actions. Acting on negative feelings in destructive ways led to Cain's sin.

Jealousy is a very human emotion. We all feel it to some degree in some area of our lives. I feel a sense of jealousy, for example, when I see friends playing golf several times a week. Though I'm an avid golfer, my schedule prohibits me from playing that often. I covet the opportunity to play as often as they. But it would be irrational of me to try to keep up with them. If I were to throw my appointment book to the wind with a who-cares attitude, there would be serious repercussions.

God, who searches us out, hears the blood of Abel crying out from the ground and calls out to Cain: "Where is your brother?" As is typical, our gracious God gives an opportunity for confession and repentance. Tragically, Cain tries to sidestep the call with a lie and sarcastic diversion: "I do not know; am I my brother's keeper?" Just as in the story of Eden where God sought out the first man and woman, asking "Where are you?" God yearns for an honest reply when he searches for Cain. What would have happened if Cain had confessed his sin and demonstrated true repentance? We will never know; Cain chose to lie and rationalize.

Cain expects the worst for his sins of murder and lying, and he believes that banishment from the land is banishment from God and God's protection. But God is gracious. When the blood of Abel calls out from the ground for revenge, God does not oblige it. Expelling Cain from Eden, God ensures his protection with a mark "so that no one who came upon him would kill him."

Just as we are like Adam and Eve, thirsting after knowledge, we are also like Cain. We see apparent injustices all around us and wonder how God can be unfair. We are jealous of those whom God seemingly favors. And we take out our anger at God on our brothers and sisters. The story of the two brothers teaches us to be honest, to lay frustration and blame where they belong. It also tells us that there is a wide variety of gifts and talents among people, and God gives protection to them all. No matter how far away from Eden we get, God is our safety and our refuge.

## Discussion and Action

1. This story pictures three actors: God, Cain, and Abel. As you read, with whom do you identify? Why?

2. At what kind of inequity, personal or social, do you feel rage? How do you deal with that rage positively? How do you deal with it negatively? Name your jealousies. How should you deal with the way you feel?

3. Cain's question ("Am I my brother's keeper?") is intended to deflect God's probing, still it is a legitimate one. In what way are Christians responsible for others in the world? How have we used Cain's question to rationalize our neglect of the suffering of humankind?

4. Abel is the scapegoat in this story. When you are unfaithful, who do you scapegoat? When people are poor, do you ask God why people suffer or do you scapegoat the poor by saying they deserve it? Have you ever been poor? Do you blame yourself? God? others?

5. What does the Cain and Abel story tell us about revenge? How do you handle feelings of revenge in your personal

life? What in your opinion should governmental institutions and nations do about revenge?

6. On a slip of paper, write out the names of people for whom you feel a responsibility. Exchange the slip of paper with someone else in the group. Covenant to call each other during the week to see what you and your partner are doing to address your responsibilities.

# 8

# A Flood and a Rainbow
### *Genesis 6:5—9:17*

*The story of the great flood reveals as much about God as it does about human nature. It depicts a disappointed God starting over when plans for the creation, especially humankind, do not work out the way they were designed. We are especially shaken by the image of a God who grieves and wants to "uncreate" the world. But we are finally relieved by a new promise, a new covenant of grace, that ends the story.*

## Personal Preparation

1. Read the genealogy in chapter 5. Note how the genealogy shows the development of civilization and the spread of sin.
2. Genesis 6:5—9:17 forms a formidable block of material, much of it familiar, some not. Intentionally read it in one sitting. Keep a note pad close by and record new insights that come to you. Be prepared to share these during the session.
3. The biblical text raises some troubling questions about God's relationship to human sin. Rethink what you believe about God and natural disaster. Does God send disaster for a purpose? for revenge? How does this story fit into your belief?
4. Think about some natural disasters that have occurred recently. Hurricane Iniki hit our lovely Hawaiian islands

as I was writing this study. How would you react to this disaster in relationship to your theology? Why are some spared and others not?

## Understanding

A story has it that a butcher named Mulligan had a regular tee time with three other buddies during the work week. He barely had enough time to doff his working clothes, don his golfing wear, get into his car, and drive out to the course. By the time he got there, the other three would already be making their way to the first tee. He quickly put on his golf shoes, picked up his clubs, and hustled out to join them. When it was his chance to tee off, of course, he did not have the same opportunity to warm up as the others. Often his first several shots were poor, reflecting his lack of preparedness. So, in order to even things out, the other three players agreed to give him one grace shot off the first tee if he wanted it. And so the practice of "taking a Mulligan" had its beginning.

All of us have, at some point in life, wanted the opportunity to have a second chance. Surprisingly, God took a similar second chance. The familiar story of the great flood begins when God regrets having made the world (6:6-7). The divine eyes see a world dominated by sin (6:5), faithlessness, and the gift of freedom gone awry. The thought that God would rue the day the world was made is so startling that the writer repeats it. God was sorry for having made the creation. The God we trust when we are in the depth of despair wanted to scrap the divine plan and start over.

When we think about it, we realize that this passage raises questions about God's power. Did or did not God have control over how the world would turn out? The answer has tremendous implications for how we understand God and how we believe God relates to the world. The biblical image of God that we rely on most shows God as omnipotent and immutable. In other words, God has the power to do anything and know everything past, present, and future.

But this passage reveals another picture of God. (And it is not the only picture in the scriptures that offers a contradictory image of God.) It depicts a God who is willing to give humans some freedom to make their own choices and determine their own futures. God truly hopes for goodness and faithfulness. But in their freedom, humankind chooses sin. Sin begets sin, and soon sin dominates creation.

Certainly, this sin did not fit into the divine hope for the creation. The dominance of sin caused God to be sorrowful and repentant. It makes me wonder if God would be sorrowful today? Is God disappointed in ethnic cleansing? the Holocaust? apartheid? Surely heaven's tears must come from godly sorrow over these and other contemporary sins.

God sorrowing is surely a lesser theme in biblical literature. More often the Bible sings hearty amens to the words of the hymn:

> We blossom and flourish as leaves on the tree,
> And wither and perish, but naught changeth Thee.

But the passage upon which we focus today does not stand alone in the scripture. See, for example, Genesis 18:16-33; Exodus 32:7-14; and Hosea 11. These passages paint portraits of a God who is open to change and hears human intercession, a God who created the world for goodness and is deeply pained when events go the other direction. Although the image of a powerful, all-knowing God is the dominant one in the Bible, I personally find comfort in the biblical image of a changeable God who hears and responds. It is a sign that God relates to us and hears us and that our choice to be faithful is pleasing.

When we understand God to be a suffering, compassionate God, we see that God can be touched by human action and petition. This understanding makes prayer more hopeful, especially when we plead on behalf of ourselves and others. We can offer our prayers with the constant hope that God will hear and be open to the possibility of change. If, in God's grand view, all things for all eternity are determined, our petitions would not mean much. Prayers of intercession do make a difference.

The flood story also contains another theme: judgment through destruction. God grieves and wills the destruction of all the earth. We cannot avoid this theme even though it stands alongside a description of God as compassionate. Like the destruction of Sodom (Gen. 19:12-29) and Jerusalem (2 Kgs. 24), God is seen as responsible for bringing judgment in the form of death for unrepentant sinners.

How do we deal with this hard word? We cannot do an easy two-step around the beliefs of the author of Genesis. I find Old

Testament scholar Bruce Vawter's explanation in *On Genesis* most satisfying. Vawter contends that the story of the flood was a familiar one to Near Eastern peoples. Various cultures had myths about a great flood that wiped out the world (except for one remaining hero). But in those versions, it was an amoral and capricious god who brought the rains. Vawter says:

> In the Mesopotamian stories of the flood, no real motivation is ever offered to explain why the gods brought about this particular disaster. . . . In the biblical story the divine motivation for the flood is of its essence. What the Bible has done is to turn an amoral myth into a highly moral parable of God's retribution and grace responding to the challenge of his creatures' willfulness and evildoing. There and there alone lies the biblical message intended by the flood story.

God informs Noah of his intentions to destroy creation. Noah is chosen to survive because he is "a righteous man, blameless in his generation." This description stands in contrast to the rest of humankind, whose "inclination of the thoughts of their hearts was only evil continually" (6:5). The heart in Hebrew understanding was the seat of human life. It represented all that life held, physically, mentally, emotionally, and spiritually. By associating sin with the heart, the author gives us a completely base picture of humankind. Evil reigned.

Note that not only is humankind destroyed because of sin, but also "people together with animals and creeping things and birds of the air. . . ." When humankind sins, other parts of the creation suffer as well. Is this not true in all times everywhere? The environment provides the most obvious example. Because of human folly, all creation suffers. And God grieves.

God is not angry or vengeful in the story of the flood. God is sad and decides to wipe away the dismal first creation. To adapt the words of Jesus, "The rains came, and the winds blew and beat on the earth, and great was the fall of it." The order of creation was reversed. Whereas creation brought life from chaos and void, the flood returned creation to void: "[God] blotted out every living thing that was on the face of the ground, human beings and animals and creeping things and birds of the air; they were blotted out from the earth" (7:23).

All except Noah and the inhabitants of the ark, that is! After 190 days—40 of rain and 150 following—the floods subside. The dove goes forth to pluck the olive leaf. God still wants to fulfill the covenant. God still wants creation, but an alternative creation. There is still the command to "be fruitful and multiply," but the story makes much of the fact that the second "first" family, headed by Noah, is obedient, unlike the family in the garden. God hopes that the second creation will not use its freedom to cause pain and grief, but will fulfill the divine purpose of creation. As a sign of the new covenant, God sets an arc in the sky. Every time the rainbow appears after a storm, it reminds the people of God's promise to them and their responsibility to obey and be faithful.

Once again, the scripture sounds the theme that is central in all of the stories of our faith: God is all-powerful. God is all-powerful in the sense that God uses all ways to bring the world in line with the divine will. And God does so because in the end God is gracious, compassionate, and relational, wanting to cover sin with grace and save us, even when we resist.

## Discussion and Action

1. Discuss the idea that scripture reveals a God open to persuasion and change. Talk about some of the scriptures that show God changing. How does that fit with or contradict your understanding of God?
2. Discuss your feeling about God's power to destroy. Even though you live under the covenant given to Noah, what feelings do you have about God's destructive act in this text?
3. Consider that sin persists today. Although God has promised not to destroy, how do we live under the judgment of our actions anyway? How is the rest of creation being affected by our sin?
4. Share your beliefs about the covenant promise God gives and the symbol of the rainbow. In what ways do you claim that promise in your life today?
5. Close with the hymn "Amazing Grace," with one person reading the words in a stanza followed by the group singing the words.

---

# 9

---

# God Scatters a People
## *Genesis 11:1-9*

*The story of the tower of Babel is often used to explain
how the peoples of the earth came to have different
languages. In this session we look at what the story says
about God's plan to multiply and fill the world and the
people's fear of spreading out to cover the face of the
earth.*

## Personal Preparation

1. Read Genesis 9:18—10:32, the postdeluvian (post-flood)
   passages which precede the tower of Babel story. Look for
   the themes of disobedience and faithfulness in 9:18-29.
   Also ponder the significance of Noah's genealogy, which
   makes up chapter 10.
2. Read Genesis 11:1-9. The previous stories with which we
   have dealt reveal human sin: disobedience, lying, murder,
   and the like. What sin(s) is (are) central to the story of the
   tower of Babel?
3. On the surface, the story of the tower of Babel is about
   language. Reflect on how people who speak the same
   language often fail to understand each other. When do
   people speak different languages and still communicate?
4. This story holds implications for prayer. In prayer, we not
   only speak to God, we also listen to God to understand the
   divine will. If we are silent in the presence of the Holy, we
   can know what to do. Amid all the confusion of human

voices, God's voice can reach us in prayer. Take time in silence this week to hear God's voice as you search for clarity on some personal or social problem.

## Understanding

Have you ever pondered how varied languages are? As a would-be musician, I enjoy singing in Italian and Hawaiian, because most of the words in these languages end in vowels, making them much easier to sing than German, for example. Some languages, such as Greek, are extraordinarily logical, while others, such as English, defy consistency and rules.

And as a self-proclaimed film critic, I like to watch foreign films in the screenwriter's language. *Rashomon* from Japan and *Das Boot* from Germany stand out as favorites, even though I spend a lot of energy the first time around focusing on the subtitles and sometimes fail to catch the significance of the whole film.

A single language, such as English, is made even more colorful by dialects and accents, as well as different spellings or words for the same object. Languages add to the richness of cultures. On the other hand, the existence of different languages can also create difficulty and confusion. We may fear traveling abroad because our inability to speak other languages isolates us from people. Even if we do know a second language, we rarely know it as well as our native tongue. Something is always lost in the translation. This session focuses in part on the biblical account of the creation of languages and culture and on our feelings of separation and isolation because of language. Its main purpose, however, is to encourage us to scatter with God's message and to resist the temptation of staying with our "own kind."

The story of the tower of Babel has a fablelike quality. The New English Bible begins the story "Once upon a time . . ." as if it is a parable rather than a historical account. We are being told why rather than how something came to be. Why, do you suppose, are there now distinct and different groupings of people when creation began with a single family in a specific location? Well, once upon a time . . .

The passage may be separated into two distinct parts: the human attempt to build the tower (vv. 1-4) and God's reaction and response (vv. 5-9). Let's take a look at both aspects of the story.

**Let's make a name for ourselves (vv. 1-4).** The teller sets the scene in Mesopotamia by using the words "brick . . . and bitumen," common building materials unique to that location. Furthermore, the name of the tower, Babel, is probably derived from Babylon, the name of the city in Mesopotamia.

In this setting, we are told how the whole earth had one language. Literally, the Hebrew says "one lip." Obviously, the teller wants to cast this story in prehistory, when all people were descended from common stock in a direct line. The genealogy of Noah and his three sons immediately preceding this story emphasizes that all of humankind was united as a family.

In the story, humankind wants to build a city with its "tower in the heavens," as a landmark by which they will all be known and identified as their society multiplies and spreads out: "let us make a name for ourselves; otherwise we will be scattered" (v. 4). To make themselves known, they built a tower that would elevate them to a level near to God.

In both ancient and modern civilizations, people have identified high places with the dwelling place of God. In the biblical tradition alone, we can readily identify Mount Sinai, Hermon, Zion, and the Mount of the Transfiguration as examples. But we can as readily see the quest for high places today. A few years ago, when I lived in the San Francisco area, a Christian sect decided that on a specific day Jesus would come again. After selling all their worldly possessions, they congregated on a mountaintop just outside San Francisco to await the Lord, as if by going up the mountain, the people could save Jesus a few steps!

Even church architecture points symbolically upward to the place of God who transcends the world. Arched windows, steep cathedral ceilings and needlelike spires direct our eyes and our thoughts heavenward. Although most of us have given up the ancient belief that God exists "up there," we still look to the skies when imagining God's abode. The psalmist sings: "I lift up my eyes to the hills—from where will my help come? My help comes from the Lord . . ." (Psa. 121:1-2). Ancient Mesopotamians were no different. They created their ziggurat, a stepped pyramidlike structure that would carry them upward, not only to meet God, but to become like God, transcending their earthly confines.

Building the tower had two effects. First of all, the people succeeded in making a name for themselves and were bold about establishing themselves as godlike. On the other hand, they feared being scattered abroad upon the face of the earth and believed this project would keep that from happening. The former reminds us of the theme of the garden, wherein the primal pair wanted to be like God (3:5). The latter is an obvious transgression of the divine intention to multiply and fill the earth.

**God responds (vv. 5-8).** God's response to the people's ambition to be godlike and their resistance to going out into the world is like the divine response to the first sin of Adam and Eve (3:1f). When God discovered their sin, he put the couple out of the garden—scattered from their home with God. In the story of the tower, we can almost hear again the surprise in God's initial response. After contemplating and spelling out the possible consequences of the deed (v. 6), God acts decisively to frustrate the human act (vv. 7-8). Only this time God wants the people to spread abroad. The "punishment" is really the fulfillment of God's original intent. The establishment of many languages would make the people scatter.

One would think that this human attempt to stay together would be the appropriate response to the divine intent for unity. Why is this not so? After all, is this not the vision of the New Testament, that is, that all may be one (John 17:21; Gal. 3:28)?

Perhaps God objected to their effort because the people misunderstood that they must both unify and scatter. They must be of one purpose—faithfulness, but they must carry their faithfulness over the earth by scattering themselves. It was human folly for them to think they could reach God out of their own devices and initiative.

Likewise, rather than God responding to our initiative, God wants us to respond to the divine initiative. Whether by divine covenant established in the desert, as we will see in the next session, or through the New Covenant established by Jesus, which we find revealed in the gospel, we can only reach God on God's terms.

This story is one of many that tells us that God's will is for the people to scatter, to go and tell. It is also a story that typifies human arrogance and hubris in thinking we can do our own thing, including taking charge of the universe. Whenever we dare to do so, God thwarts our intentions one way or another and leaves open only one option—to have faith in God's redeeming work and initiative: "By grace are you saved through faith . . . it is not your own doing . . . ."

## Discussion and Action

1. What sins are central to the tower of Babel story?

2. This Bible passage reveals how humans try to manufacture ways to be godlike. Share examples from contemporary society and from your own life in which humankind has tried to take control. How has God thwarted these intentions?

3. This story, with its emphasis on different languages as a way to keep people scattered, can be contrasted with the experience at Pentecost in Acts 2. There, the people speak different languages but can understand each other. What linkages do you find between the tower of Babel story and Pentecost? How are they different?

4. How does God "punish" our prideful attempts to control life? How does God help us to know divine love and grace? How does God provide that knowledge for you personally.

5. What would it take for you to be willing to go abroad with God's message? Or are you are more inclined to minister where you are? Why? How do we show Christian unity with people in other places who speak other languages and do things differently?

6. End with silent prayer, listening for the voice of God directing your life. Close the prayer, singing "Kum ba yah."

# 10

## Beginning Again
### *Genesis 11:10—12:3*

*Our final session is really the beginning. The story of Abraham and Sarah is where the story of God's family starts. The first 11 chapters of Genesis are a faith statement that tells why God created the world. In Abraham we will see how God created a people of faith.*

## Personal Preparation

1. Reflect on the past nine weeks. What insights or new learnings stand out for you? List them on a piece of paper, and take some time in prayer to give thanks to God for giving you new understanding.
2. Genesis 12 marks the transition into a considerably different way of looking at events. Up to this point in Genesis, we have been looking at the beginning of the world in all its expanse. Suddenly, in Genesis 12, we are reading the story of Abraham and Sarah and their descendants. Read Genesis 11:10—12:3 carefully to see how the transition is made.
3. Since this is a new beginning, compare this "creation" story with the creation stories in Genesis 1 and 2. Do you see some common themes?

## Understanding

A great deal has happened in the biblical drama since we watched God create the world on the stage of the universe. We saw the Divine make the world and everything in it and announce that "it is good." We thrust our chests out in pride as God created humankind at the height of the created order and gave us the role of steward over the rest of creation. Our shoulders hunched forward as we saw the primordial pair misuse their God-given freedom in order to disobey God and thereby introduce sin into the creation. Tears filled our eyes as we saw hatred, murder, lies, rationalizations, and all kinds of evil fill a sin-sick world. We could do nothing as God concluded that it would be better to start from scratch and then wiped out all of creation in a flood. But even that drastic act did not eliminate sin. The tower of Babel gave dramatic proof of that. It is a worsening account that we have heard so far.

If the tower of Babel signaled the end of the story, we would be, to paraphrase Paul, of all people the most miserable. But thankfully the story revolves around a God who saves. As Paul Harvey says, "And now for the rest of the story." Interestingly, "the rest of the story" is older than the stories of creation. Before Adam and Eve, before Noah and the tower of Babel, the Hebrews were recounting the history of their ancestor Abraham and God's promise to provide heirs. But when the Bible was written down, the recorders of Genesis put the grand story of first things first. It makes more sense to start with the drama of creation, followed by the scattering of whole nations, and then a close-up story of one family. In reading the story of Abraham as the beginning of the human family of faith, we look backward at creation and forward into the history of Israel.

This point is important, for the genealogy which serves as a transition between the first 11 chapters and the remaining chapters of Genesis focuses on Abraham. The names that precede his serve to link him with what has been told before. Why is the call of Abraham of such crucial importance? Precisely because Abraham stands at the beginning of the long journey in which God saves us and calls humankind to be the family of faith.

The writer subtly begins reciting the story of how God saved the world—so subtly you may not have noticed. From 11:10 to 11:26, we see a straightforward genealogy that links Noah's son Shem to Abraham. Then in verses 27-30, the story picks up and we learn a few details of Abraham's family, including the fact that "Sarah was barren; she had no child" (v. 30). We have heard this promise before, that God will create something from nothing. We are hooked and we read on.

The fact that Sarah was childless has two important implications. The first is that somehow we are going to get numerous progeny from a barren woman. We will explore this later. The second is that the birth of Isaac will be a miracle. This implication cannot be explored fully, for that story stands outside this study. It is sufficient to say, at this point, that all the events making up the story of God's covenant with Abraham are filled with the signs of God's intervening power and love. Things happened as they did only because God ordained them so.

Taking a closer look at the covenant itself, we see that it consists of two parts: the call to go (12:1) and the promises of good things that will ensue if the covenant is fulfilled (12:2-3). In the call, God tells Abraham to leave the security of his home and a life of relative ease for the unknown. God does not even bother to point out the destination to Abraham. Though Abraham knew what nomadic life was like, he must have been struck by the radical nature of a call that had no goal. There is much risk here.

Many people have ventured forth in faith, leaving security behind. Albert Schweitzer was a venturesome person and a great inspiration for me. Schweitzer was at the height of his career as a scientist when he announced he would leave it to serve as a missionary doctor in Africa. When he told his friends, they were shocked. After all, Schweitzer was a respected physician, world-renowned organist, teacher, theologian, author. Why would he throw away all of that to go and live in primitive conditions.

On one occasion, a confidant came to Schweitzer and shared people's speculations. Some were saying he was leaving because of a broken love affair. Others guessed Schweitzer was in financial trouble. A flurry of rumors ran rampant. After hearing this report, Schweitzer shook his head in dismay and asked, "Can they not understand that Jesus is calling me?"

The promises accompanying the call to Abraham do not necessarily comfort him. They are filled with unknowns and generalities. I wonder if Abraham did not feel he was being tricked here! He must have heard the promise of progeny with some skepticism. After all, his wife could not bear children. How could God make him father of a great nation of people?

Furthermore, the promise that others would be blessed through Abraham may not have lent much comfort, either. According to Jewish understanding, the promise of blessing consisted primarily of material increase, that is, offspring. In the end, all parts of the blessing centered on the promise of heirs, making the rather offhand comment about Sarah being barren more significant.

We know from our perspective thousands of years later that God was true to those promises. Would we have had the faith that Abraham, who knew nothing, had to follow God's command? The truth is that we limit God when we confine him to what *we* regard as possible. We can all attest to this truth. God took the void and brought about the magnificence of the creation, and God can take the barren places in our lives and bring about abundant and eternal life. Paul quotes scripture, saying: " 'What no eye has seen, nor ear heard, what God has prepared for those who love him'—these things God has revealed to us through the Spirit" (1 Cor. 2:9). When we trust God's ability to fulfill divine promises, we will see and hear things we cannot even imagine. Anyone who has done so can testify to that truth.

One summer, our congregation had to trust God to lead us out of chaos when tragedy struck our youth group. On the final day of their annual summer retreat, the youth were returning home when the driver of one of the vans in which they were traveling fell asleep at the wheel, causing an accident. A girl from our youth group was killed. The whole congregation grieved deeply, but God's gracious hand loved us all through the process and brought healing. Her parents especially, as you would imagine, felt the emptiness and void left by her death. But an inner beauty has arisen out of the grave of death, a beauty we could not have foreseen in the chaos.

In faith, we let God lead us, as did Abraham. Abraham's obedient response stands in contrast to the acts of disobedience that characterize the earlier stories in Genesis, especially the story of original sin. Just as disobedience led to sin and death, the obedience of Abraham leads to salvation.

As the New Testament points out, however, the one characteristic of Abraham that stands out more than obedience is faith (Heb. 11:8-12). Paul goes so far as to say that the true descendants of Abraham are not the children of his flesh but those who emulate his faith in God (Rom. 9:6f.). The point is this: God is a God who calls. Even as we are called, God helps us to fulfill our calling and blesses us in the process. God has given us Abraham as an example of one who was faithful and encourages us to respond in the same way.

This is an encouraging, hopeful word after the disappointments of Genesis 3—11. Just as God's call and promise were issued to Abraham in the midst of a sinful and barren world, we hope that God will call us and we will hear the call over the sin and chaos of our time. So, we are left with grace and hope. Consistently, God has demonstrated that grace is a divine characteristic. In each of the creation stories, God refuses to leave the actors to their sins. God comes seeking and saving. How can we doubt that this will hold true for us as well? How indeed!

## Discussion and Action

1. The author sees faith as the center of Abraham. What are some of the characteristics of that faith? How is that kind of faith a part of your life? Are there areas of your life where you need an increase in faith?

2. Can you relate to the story of God calling Abraham into the unknown? When have you felt the divine call? How did you respond? What happened as a result of your obeying or not obeying the call?

3. In creation, God brings order out of chaos. How has God brought order out of chaos in your life?

4. Think of all the creation stories we have studied: Genesis 1—2, Noah, Abraham, and Jesus. Has God stopped creating? How is God still creating? What would make God want to start over? Who would be the modern Noah or Abraham?

5. Here is a possible order of worship for closing.

    Call to Worship:
    Psalm 119:103-105

    Opening Prayer

    Hymn:
    "God of Grace and God of Glory"

    Celebration through Sharing:
    Share insights and new life gained
    through this study.

    Hymn:
    "There Is Wideness in God's Mercy"

    Closing Prayer

# Suggestions for Sharing and Prayer

This material is designed for covenant groups that spend one hour in sharing and praying together, in addition to the hour of Bible study. The suggestions offered here will help to relate the group's sharing to the study of *In the Beginning*. Session-by-session ideas are given first, followed by general resources. Use those that are best suited to your group, and bring your own ideas for sharing and worshiping together. June Adams Gibble, of Elgin, Illinois, and Suzanne DeMoss Martin, of Indianapolis, Indiana, compiled this guide.

## 1. In the Beginning

☐ Take time to begin forming your covenant group, using the suggestions found in the General Sharing and Prayer Resources section: Forming a Covenant Group. The People of the Covenant theme song, "Weave," may also be used; it can be found in other Covenant Bible studies: *Covenant People* and *Mystery and Glory in John's Gospel*.

☐ Before your meeting ask people to bring family photo albums and share some important family photos. Talk about how each photo is important to your family's early history or beginnings and the meaning it holds for you today.

☐ Use the hymn "Lord, Listen to Your Children" (p. 62) for your prayer time.

    a. Pray silently as one person reads the words as a call to prayer. Or one or two people may sing the hymn as a call to prayer.

    b. Then let the leader read the first phrase of the hymn with the group repeating the words; continue through the hymn.

    c. Invite brief spoken prayers, asking God to be present as you begin your group life; also invite personal prayer requests.

    d. Close by singing the hymn through once or twice. Or read
    the words again.

## 2. And It Was Good!

❑ Share times from childhood or youth when you were struck
by an awareness of the goodness of God's creation.

❑ Name hymns about God's creation that have been important
to you. How have they been a part of your faith journey?
Sing some of these together.

❑ Look through hymnals for hymns about creation—of the
earth, of people, of the new creation. Share some of the
phrases or stanzas that speak to you and your faith today.
Again, enjoy singing some of these.

❑ Discover the power in this creation story (Gen. 1—2:4a),
giving special attention to the poetry and the repetition of
phrases. Here are two possibilities (to be used alone or
combined into one reading):

    a. Using the same translation of the Bible, let all but two
    people read the narrator's part of the text, with two people
    reading together the words of God.

    b. Use an echo effect in the reading to symbolize creation
    coming into being. One or two voices could read the text,
    pausing after particular words (*earth* [v. 1], *deep*, *waters*
    [v. 2], *light* [v. 3], *good* [v. 4], *Day*, *Night* [v. 5], *day*
    [v. 6]) with each person around the group repeating that
    word, creating an echo effect. Use this echo for key words
    throughout the text—including *good* ("It was good") and
    *so* ("And it was so") each time these phrases occur. The
    last echo-word will be *created* (2:4a).

❑ Recognize that, as you are reading and hearing these familiar
words, you are praying the scriptures.

❑ Use the hymn "I Sing the Mighty Power of God" (p.63) as a
closing prayer, reading the words together as your prayer of
praise to God.

## 3. Remember the Sabbath

☐ Invite one or two people from your parents' or grandparents' generation to share sabbath memories and practices from years ago. Or share stories of sabbath you heard from your own parents and grandparents.

☐ Recall the words of an old hymn: "Oh come to the church in the wildwood, oh come to the church in the vale. . . . How sweet on a clear Sabbath morning to list to the clear ringing bell." If some group members know this hymn, you may want to sing it.

☐ Share your first memories of going to church or being in a church worship service.

☐ Note that at the end of creation God rested and enjoyed the creation (Gen. 2:1-3). Share times when you are able just to rest and enjoy creation, or times when you have been forced to rest, for example, because of a snowstorm or recovery from surgery.

☐ Move into a time of quiet meditation, using these words from a prayer hymn:

> O Sabbath rest by Galilee!
> O calm of hills above,
> where Jesus knelt to share with thee
> the silence of eternity,
> interpreted by love;
>
> Drop thy still dews of quietness,
> till all our strivings cease.
> Take from our souls the strain and stress,
> and let our ordered lives confess
> the beauty of thy peace.

a. First, be in silent prayer.

b. Then have one person sing (or speak) these words prayerfully, moving at the same time from person to person, gently placing hands on each one's head. Continue until all have been blessed with the laying on of hands. Then a group member may want to lay hands in blessing on the speaker/singer's head.

c. If you know the tune, you may want to quietly sing the hymn together, with a closing "Amen."

## 4. In God's Image

❑ Find a copy of the book *God's Trombones* by James Weldon Johnson (out of print but available in many pastors', church, or public libraries). Have one person dramatically read or speak this well-known African American sermon. Invite people to share their feelings in response to this reading. Then discuss what this very intimate and personal portrayal says about being created "in God's image."

❑ Create symbols of your relationship with God as it is right now (thinking of the ups, the downs, the questions, the struggles, the affirmations, the hopes). You will need paper, pens, crayons, yarn, scissors, and similar items for writing poetry or prayers and making art objects or symbols. When all are finished, talk about the symbols and their meanings.

❑ Close your sharing time by offering sentence prayers to God and singing stanza 4 of "God of the Earth, the Sky, the Sea" (p. 64).

## 5. Man and Woman

❑ Talk about your first memories of this creation story (found in Gen. 2). In your sharing, have each person who is willing, finish these sentences: "At that time, I believed . . . " and "At that time, I asked these questions . . . . "

❑ As you've studied this text this week, what insights do you have? Have any questions arisen? What is the main truth in this creation story?

❑ This creation account emphasizes the importance of relationship. So do the words of the hymn "Help Us to Help Each Other" (p. 65). Read the words together as a prayer of intercession.

❑ Ask each person to name a prayer wish or concern. Then pray for each other, with each one praying aloud for the person on the right. Continue around the circle and close with the Lord's Prayer or by singing "Spirit of the Living God."

## 6. In the Garden

❑ Recall some first-time experiences from your adolescence (learning to drive, a first date). Talk about the excitement, pain, or risk. Were you disobeying any "rules" or testing any limits? What did you learn through that experience?

❑ Let prayer time center on prayers of confession. Select from the following:

a. Pray with a prayer partner. Have each person in silent prayer write down their confession of sin or omission and share it with the partner. Then one person places hands on the other's head and prays the Lord's Prayer for that person; add a personal prayer if desired, asking for forgiveness and healing. Repeat with the other person.

b. In the total group, ask people to write down ways we participate in corporate or global wrongdoing. Read these aloud reflectively and prayerfully; then pray together the Lord's Prayer and sing "Amazing Grace." As you sing, you may want to put the papers in a container and burn them, or tear them into small pieces and throw them into a wastebasket.

c. Pray the scriptures, using Psalm 51:1-4, 10-12. Have each person read verses 1-4 silently, as a confessional prayer to God. Then read verses 10-12 aloud. After time for silent prayer, join in singing the first stanza of "Amazing Grace." Conclude by speaking these words to each other: "In the name of Jesus Christ, we are forgiven. Amen."

## 7. Where Is Your Brother?

❑ Think about sibling rivalry in your family. Do you recall being jealous or feeling unfairly treated? Invite people to share as they choose.

❑ Think globally. Where do you see jealousies or "sibling rivalry" between nations? or between groups within a nation? Think of ways in which you as a group could respond to global brothers and sisters, and choose one or two ways as an action project.

❑ Spend some time learning the hymn "Help Us to Help Each Other" (p. 65) so you will be able to sing it as a prayer.

❑ Pray for God's people around the world. Use some prayers from the book *A World at Prayer: The New Ecumenical Prayer Cycle* (see Recommended Resources, p. ix). Or pray sentence prayers for specific people and/or current situations of concern. Close by singing the prayer hymn "Help Us to Help Each Other."

## 8. A Flood and a Rainbow

❑ Recall and share your earliest childhood memories of this story of the flood and the rainbow (including some of its humorous aspects, such as sounds, sights, smells).

❑ Tell about the most beautiful or memorable rainbows you have seen. What feelings did they evoke?

❑ Share some personal and family experiences with natural disasters. How have you experienced God's presence and promise at such times?

❑ Recall the hymn "Standing On the Promises of God," having someone share the words and perhaps singing it as a group.

❑ Name some ways your church has responded to natural disasters around the world. Invite people who have participated in disaster response programs to share with you. Is there some response your group would like to make?

❑ Close with prayer. You could sing the hymn "O God Our Help in Ages Past" as a prayer. Or pray the Lord's Prayer in this way: Read Matthew 6:9b-13 aloud, using different translations of the Bible. Beware of the slightly different words and phrases, the varied voices and nuances of expression. Pray silently for brothers and sisters around the world. Close by praying the Lord's Prayer in the words you usually use and/or by singing "Lord, Listen to Your Children" (p. 62).

## 9. God Scatters a People

❑ Bring some type of building materials (Tinker Toys, Lego blocks, Lincoln Logs, Blockhead game) to the group. Together construct a tower, as tall as possible (you may want to do this without speaking). Discuss what happened. What helped your building? How did you work together? What does this tell you about how you have come together as a covenant group in these eight weeks?

❑ Do a "gifts bombardment," naming all the gifts a person brings to the group. Bombard each person in the group in turn. Have the person on the right keep time (1 or 2 minutes each) and the person on the left write the gift list.

❑ Close by reading aloud one person's gifts, with all responding "Hear our prayer of thanks for _____ , O God."
Continue around the whole group, <sub>(name)</sub>
reading each person's gift list and responding with the prayer of thanks. Close by giving everyone their gift lists.

❑ Share information and prayers from different countries, found in *A World at Prayer: The New Ecumenical Prayer Cycle.* (See Recommended Resources, p. ix.)

## 10. Beginning Again

❑ Remember your first meeting as a covenant group. What were your feelings? What did you look forward to? What felt scary or risky then?

❑ Genesis 1—11 is full of beginnings. Our lives have many beginnings also, some joyful, some painful, some hopeful. Share some of your beginnings. As you finish this Bible study, how is it a beginning?

❑ One person said, "God embraced us with the creation. It was given to us as a gift, and God said, 'Wow!' " Share some recent times when you experienced God's gift of creation and said "Wow!"

❑ Enjoy recalling the biblical stories you've studied. Ask each person to name a favorite one and share new insights into that story and the meaning it has had for his or her life.

❑ Join in a closing prayer time. You may want to write a "Prayer for New Beginnings" as a group and pray it together for closure. Or use the hymn "Kum ba yah" as a prayer, singing "Come by here, my Lord, come by here. . . . Someone's crying. . . . singing. . . . praying." You can add verses, thinking of phrases of eight syllables, for example: ("Keep us faithful, Lord, to your word" or "Keep your children, Lord, in your love" or "Help us hear your call and obey").

# General Sharing and Prayer Resources

## Forming a Covenant Group

Covenant-making is an important part of the biblical story. God made covenants with the people, beginning with Noah and Abram. Many of the prophets spoke of broken covenants and the need for renewing covenant; Jesus called people to new understandings of the covenant with God. He also called the early church to be in covenant with God and with each other.

As Christians today, we also covenant with God and with each other. These covenant commitments help us live out our faith. As we come together in small covenant groups to share, pray, study God's word, and seek to live our faith, the Spirit's presence empowers us to live out covenants.

As a beginning covenant group, you will make commitments with each other. Ask yourselves these questions to help you decide about the kinds of commitments that will guide your group life:

- What are our hopes, fears, expectations for this covenant group?

- What are our expectations about being present at all meetings? How will we handle unavoidable absences?

- How can we help each person participate fully in our sharing and prayer time? in our Bible study?

- How will we work together to build trust? How can we work at keeping confidences?

- What are the important areas of congregational life for each of us? How will we continue to participate fully in the congregation's life and work?

The burlap cross has become the symbol of covenant groups. Its imperfections, the rough texture and unrefined fabric, the interweaving of threads, the uniqueness of each strand, are elements which are present within the covenant group. The people in the groups are imperfect, unpolished, interrelated with each other, yet still unique beings.

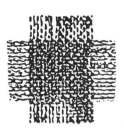

The shape that this collection of imperfect threads creates is the cross, symbolizing for all Christians the resurrection and presence of Christ our Savior. A covenant group is something akin to this burlap cross. It unites common, ordinary people and sends them out again in all directions to be in the world.

## A Litany of Commitment

All:    We are a people of the covenant;
Out of our commitment to Christ,
    we seek to become:

Group 1:    more biblically informed
    so we understand better God's revelation;

Group 2:    more globally aware
    so we know ourselves connected
    with all of God's people;

Group 1:    more relationally sensitive to God, self, and others.

All:    We are a people of the covenant;
We promise:

Group 2:    to seek ways of living out and sharing our faith;

Group 1:    to participate actively in congregational life;

Group 2:    to be open to the leading of the Spirit in our lives.

All:    We are a people of the covenant;
We commit ourselves:

Group 1:    to attend each group meeting, so far as possible;

Group 2:    to prepare through Bible study, prayer, and action;

Group 1:    to share thoughts and feelings, as appropriate;

Group 2:     to encourage each other on our faith journeys.

All:          We are a people of the covenant.

> [The preceding information and Litany of Commitment are from the
> People of the Covenant program, Church of the Brethren
> General Board, 1451 Dundee Avenue, Elgin, Illinois 60120.]

**A Covenant Prayer**

O God, we renew the covenant,
spoken by our fathers and mothers,
    sung in homes and meeting houses,
    written by the pens of pilgrims and preachers.
This covenant we know is costly;
    but there is nothing of greater value.
So we accept your gifts and promises
    with thanksgiving;
And offer you our lives and our love. Amen.

> By Leland Wilson. Adapted from *The Gifts We Bring,* Vol. 2.
> Church of the Brethren General Board, Elgin, Ill.

## Hymns and Scriptures About God's Creation

As a group project during these ten weeks, keep a growing list
of hymns and scripture texts that speak of God's creation. Examples
are: "Morning Has Broken," "This Is My Father's World," Job
38—41, and Isaiah 40:12-31; 65:17-25. Enjoy singing the hymns
and sharing the scriptures with each other regularly during your
sharing time.

## Resources for Praying Together

An old proverb says, "You pray twice when you sing."

❑ Use a variety of hymns as different forms of prayer (praise,
   adoration, thanksgiving, confession, intercession,
   commitment). Let your body posture reflect your prayers:
   kneeling for prayers of confession; standing in a circle or
   laying hands on one another for prayers of intercession;
   standing with hands raised or outstretched or clapping for
   prayers of praise and thanksgiving.

❑ Learn to enjoy singing by "lining out" the hymns, with one person reading or singing a phrase, followed by the group reading or singing the same phrase.

❑ Pray with a prayer hymn such as "Breathe on Me, Breath of God." Have each of four people read one stanza as prayer, with pauses between each for silent prayers. Or have one or two voices sing a stanza, followed by silent prayer; repeat through the hymn.

❑ Sing the hymn "Break Thou the Bread of Life" as a prayer before beginning Bible study, or before and following the reading of the scripture text.

❑ Establish "prayer partners" for the duration of the study. Spend some time each session praying together, and pray for each other every day during the week.

❑ Use *A World at Prayer: The New Ecumenical Prayer Cycle* to guide your Covenant group's prayer life, with each person praying the prayers at home during the week, and the group praying them together. Consider beginning in the fall and using this prayer guide throughout the year.

## A Guideline for Studying Genesis Stories

1. Remember how and where you first heard the story and any songs, games, or activities related to it.
2. Share your memories; then complete the following:
   In the beginning, I believed . . .

   In the beginning, I asked these questions . . .

3. Then read the story aloud.
4. Identify any current images, songs, interpretations related to the story.
5. When you hear this story now, what questions arise?
6. What new insights have you discovered?
7. What is the "capital T" (TRUTH) in the story, both for you personally and for all people?

# Lord, Listen to Your Children

*CHILDREN PRAYING 98.99*

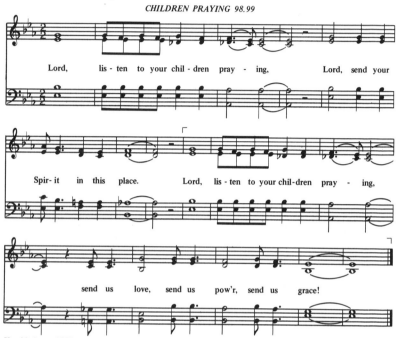

Lord, lis - ten to your chil - dren pray - ing, Lord, send your Spir- it in this place. Lord, lis - ten to your chil-dren pray - ing, send us love, send us pow'r, send us grace!

Ken Medema, 1970

# I Sing the Mighty Power of God

*ELLACOMBE CMD*

1. I sing the might-y pow'r of God, that made the moun-tains rise,
that spread the flow-ing seas a - broad and built the loft - y skies.
I sing the wis-dom that or-dained the sun to rule the day.
The moon shines full at God's com-mand and all the stars o - bey.

2. I sing the good-ness of the Lord, that filled the earth with food.
God formed the crea-tures with a word, and then pro-nounced them good.
Lord, how thy won-ders are dis-played, wher - e'er I turn my eye,
if I sur - vey the ground I tread, or gaze up - on the sky!

3. There's not a plant or flow'r be - low, but makes thy glo - ries known,
and clouds a - rise, and tem-pests blow, by or - der from thy throne.
While all that bor-rows life from thee is ev - er in thy care,
there's not a place where we can flee but God is pres - ent there.

Text:   Isaac Watts, *Divine Songs for Children,* 1715, alt.
Music: *Gesangbuch der Herzogl,* 1784; harmonized by William H. Monk, *Hymns Ancient and Modern,*
         *Appendix,* 1868.

# God of the Earth, the Sky, the Sea

*ST. CATHERINE LM with refrain*

1. God of the earth, the sky, the sea! Mak - er of all a - bove, be - low! cre - a - tion lives and moves in thee, thy pre - sent life through all doth flow.
2. Thy love is in the sun - shine's glow, thy life is in the quick - 'ning air. When light - nings flash and storm - winds blow, there is thy pow'r; thy law is there.
3. We feel thy calm at eve - ning's hour, thy gran - deur in the march of night, and when thy morn - ing breaks in pow'r, we hear thy word, "Let there be light."
4. But high - er far and far more clear, thee in our spir - it we be - hold; thine im - age and thy - self are there, th'in-dwell - ing God, pro - claimed of old.

*Refrain*

We give thee thanks, thy name we sing!! Al - might - y God, our praise we bring.

Text:   Samuel Longfellow, *Hymns of the Spirit,* 1864, alt.
Music:  Henri F. Hemy, *Crown of Jesus Music,* 1864; adapted by James G. Walton, 1874.

# Help Us to Help Each Other

*BALERMA CM*

1. Help us to help each oth - er, Lord, each oth - er's load to bear, that all may live in true ac - cord, our joys and pains to share.
2. Help us to build each oth - er up, your strength with - in us prove. In - crease our faith, con firm our hope, and fill us with your love.
3. To - geth - er make us free in - deed — your life with - in us show, and in - to you, our liv - ing Head, let us in all things grow.
4. Drawn by the mag - net of your love we find our hearts made new. Near - er each oth - er let us move, and near - er still to you.

Text: Charles Wesley, *Revised Hymns for Today's Church*
Copyright © 1982 Hope Publishing Co., Carol Stream, IL 60188.
Reprinted Under License No. 3171

## Other Covenant Bible Studies available from *faithQuest:*